Haunte
Nottinghamshire - Vol One

by
Len Moakes

ISBN 0 946404 31 3

2001

The Ghost & Legends Series

**Walk & Write Ltd.,
Unit 1, Molyneux Business Park,
Whitworth Road, Darley Dale,
Matlock, Derbyshire.
England.
DE4 2HJ**

'I would therefore willingly know if you are of the opinion that phantoms are real figures . . . . or empty vain shadows raised in our imaginations by the effect of fear?'

Pliny the Younger
Concerning Phantoms

Author's Note.

This book was originally published in 1987 since when some of the establishments referred to have changed ownership or calling. For example, the Shire Hall is now the Galleries of Justice and a tourist attraction; and where, incidentally, during the restoration work, builders claimed to have seen an apparition and experienced inexplicable happenings. Babbington Colliery has become a victim of closure.

Len Moakes, 1996.

The Nottingham Psychical Research Group wish it to be known that it has no connection or affiliation with any group or organisation with similar title or any person or persons advertising as 'psychical researchers' or 'consultants' who, by inference, might use the reputation of the Nottingham Psychical Research Group to further their aims.

Contents

The Publisher and Editor are not responsible either for the opinion expressed in this book which are entirely those of the Author, or for the references to the locations referred to therein. Readers are asked to respect to privacy and calling of the establishments referred to in the text.

INTRODUCTION

Nottinghamshire is rich in ghostlore and in this book readers can, witho stirring from the warmth of their own fireside and easy chair, encounter tl numerous phantoms which are said to haunt the county. Not content wi listing these ghost stories, it was decided that, where possible, they shou be personally investigated. It was to this end that the Nottingham Psychic Research Group was established in 1982. When reports of the paranorm are brought to our attention, we try, if possible, to find a logical ar rational explanation for these strange happenings. This we are often ab to do, but it is the ones that defy explanation which intrigue us. We do n purport to be experts in this field. Who can? But over the years we c claim to have established a reputation for honesty and integrity in o approach to, and dealings with, this subject.

This selection of ghost stories from Nottinghamshire is by no means mea to be comprehensive. Due to the nature of the subject, it would be mc unwise on our part, as a responsible body of investigators, to make pub knowledge of all the cases listed in our files. For example, certain domes properties have been sold because of alleged paranormal activity b obviously without mention of this to the new owners. In other cases v have investigated, it is the wish of principal and corroborative witness that their names be witheld and we must honour these wishes. Bearing th in mind, I have had to be circumspect in the choice of what to include this book and what to omit. Therefore, a good many of the stories ha been collated from diverse sources. I trust this will not detract from tl reader's enjoyment. If anyone feels inclined to visit any of the properties locations mentioned, I urge them most strongly to observe the proprietie to use tact and discretion, and not to bring into disrepute a subject which recognised as worthy of serious study. However, the purpose of this boo is not to prove or disprove the existence of ghosts but to entertain.

I would stress that our investigations have left us in no doubt that there a still many more stories yet to be told, and I would be more than pleased hear from anyone with an experience to relate. So . . . . . turn the ligh down low, draw your chair closer to the fire and pour yourself a s drink . . . . . then come and meet the ghosts of Nottinghamshire.

Annesley Hall - was it a Ghost?

Of all the historic buildings in Nottinghamshire my favourite is Annesley Hall, beautiful in its own mysterious and haunting way. Perhaps this affection stems from my schooldays, when a friend and I chose the hall for a local history project. One Sunday afternoon, we cycled there to be warmly received by its owner, Colonel J. N. Chaworth-Musters who gave us a conducted tour of the house together with a brief lecture on its long history and that of the Chaworth-Musters family.

The central part of the house is thought to be of Norman origin. The Chaworths lived at Annesley Hall from 1439 and were one of the oldest families in the county, having been settled in Nottinghamshire since the Conquest. Laurencius de Cadurois (Chaworth) was returned as Knight of the Shire for Nottingham to Parliament at Westminster in 1313 and in 1314 Thomas de Chaworth was summoned as a landowner to perform military service. Annesley Hall is perhaps best known for the romantic association between Mary Ann Chaworth and the poet Lord Byron, who when on holiday from Harrow, would ride over from Newstead Abbey to stroll with Mary Ann in the gardens and along the terraces. This association did not develop, for in 1806 Mary Ann married Mr. John Musters, owner of the estates and halls of Colwick and Wiverton, and the name was hyphenated to Chaworth-Musters.

Many indelible memories remain with me of that Sunday afternoon of many years ago, not only of the Colonel's kindness but also of Annesley Hall when it was occupied by a family. Dark panelling was in abundance and carved ceilings added to the ambience of quiet dignity. Deer skins covered the entrance hall floor. On the walls were many family portraits together with stags' heads and several swords, one of which belonged to Sir John Byron, an ancestor of the poet. He killed William Chaworth with this sword in a duel over 200

years ago. Sadly, Annesley Hall is no longer a family home fo
after the Colonel died it was sold by his son to the Footbal
Association in 1973. A developer is now renovating th
house.

As a setting for classic ghost stories, Annesley Hall i
without equal. The overgrown churchyard is overshadowe
by the ancient and mouldering church of All Saints. Here
moss covered tombstones lean at grotesque angles. Man
historic houses of Nottinghamshire have their ghost stories
for the most part well known, and Annesley Hall is no excep
tion with its vague allusions to a 'White Lady' said to walk th
grounds. With further research, I came across an obscur
story relating to a visit made by the Quaker poet Willian
Howitt. In 1840 he was shown a portrait of a Miss Burdett,
village girl, who many years before was employed as a servan
by 'His Lordship'. Not liking her situation, she ran away, bu
he brought her back and built a cottage for her on the estate
Soon after, she died in childbirth. On the night of her deat
her relatives came and took all the money she had saved fo
the child, and from then on it is said that her tormented spiri
haunted the grounds. A caretaker at the Hall told Howitt o
another ghost, an agile lady who, it was alleged rose from
well in the grounds at midnight to sit in a tree combing he
hair, even after a parson had been engaged to exorcise he
and after the well had been covered over. Superstitiou
nonsense? Was the caretaker indulging Howitt, telling hin
what he wanted to hear? Or is there a modicum of truth in th
stories? I invite the reader to consider the following informa
tion, contained in full in a private file.

On 16th March 1983, three members of the Nottinghan
Psychical Research Group, Major H. S. J. (Jack) Lumsden
Malcolm Crozier and myself, together with a guest 'medium
arrived shortly after 10.00pm at Annesley Hall, with th
intention of investigating paranormal activity in the locality
Shortly after arrival we were met by two local policemen whc
had been informed of our intention. It was raining heavily
and the only shelter we could find was under a large archwa
situated in a building once used as a stables and dairy. As w
waited for the rain to subside one of the policemen told us of
strange experience he had had one night at the hall. Afte

carrying out a routine check of the premises he experienced a feeling that he was not alone. He admitted that he had left in a hurry, but stressed that this was the only occasion that he had experienced anything of this nature in all the times he had patrolled the area. The police left us to reflect on this and at 10.45pm Jack and I decided to go for a walk round the grounds. On reaching the flight of steps leading to the small door on the west side of the hall we both experienced a feeling of intense coldness. On moving away from this spot all seemed normal again. We gestured to Malcolm and the 'medium' to join us and they too agreed it was inordinately cold in this area. Nothing further occurred until 12.45am., when, as we were walking along a path with the lawn to our right, we felt the atmosphere grow cold again, so cold, that Malcolm's teeth began to chatter. I noticed, at the end of the lawn near to the trees, a bright luminescent shape which drifted over the lawn. The outline resembled a women with her head bowed. The others confirmed that they too could see it clearly. The sighting lasted some 15-20 seconds before it faded amongst the trees, when the atmosphere returned to normal. We searched the area of its disappearance but found nothing, and at 1.55am we decided to leave, as the weather had deteriorated.

What did we see in the grounds of Annesley Hall that night? Was it the headlights of a car reflecting off the windows? We had observed this effect before and after the sighting. Could it be attributed to the weather causing a freak mist pattern? If that were so, how could it produce the luminosity and the drop in temperature? Or was it the knowledge that we were in a reputedly haunted place and our subconcious caused a collective hallucinatory effect? But in four people at the same time? I leave you to draw your own conclusions!

Shortly after our investigations at Annesley, Jack and I visited one of the groundsmen. He had worked there for many years. Having spent some time discussing the role of the hall in the local community and the changes he had seen over the years, we informed him of the results of our recent investigation and asked him if he had ever experienced anything similar. He had felt an atmosphere on a number of occasions. Whatever observed him bore him no malice, but approved of him as he went about his work. We told him about the article in which Howitt is told of the well from whence the ghost of the young woman is said to rise. He told us that he was asked to fill the well in by Colonel Chaworth Musters the then owner of the hall to protect his grand-children.

When Annesley Hall was purchased by the Football Association, it became part of the groundsman's duties to enter the house first thing in the morning to switch the electricity on, and it was sometimes on these occasions that he felt that he was being watched, even though the building was unoccupied.

A friend asked if he could accompany him one morning. He had lived in the village all his life but had never been to the hall. He was curious as to what it was like inside. His friend was not the kind of man given to fanciful imaginings but, once inside the hall, he became agitated and uneasy but could give no reason for it. A crash reverberated through the building causing his companion to flee in panic. He was found outside some minutes later, ashen-faced and shaking. From the moment they stepped inside the hall he had sensed that there was something watching them. The groundsman tried to pacify him with an explanation of doors slamming in gusts of wind. As his friend had closed the doors behind him, he rejected the theory. He swore that he would never go near Annesley Hall again. His first visit would be his last!

Two years later when I visited a Mrs. Eileen Cupitt in connection with hauntings in Calverton she asked me if I had ever seen a ghost. I told her of the luminescent figure described above although I did not say where I had seen it. When I had finished she said, 'That is very interesting for an acquaintance of mine once saw a figure exactly the same as you describe one night on a bridle path'.

When asked where, she replied, 'At a place not far from here called Annesley Hall'.

Bestwood Lodge Hotel

Bestwood Lodge Hotel is situated in some seventy acres of woods and parkland and yet it is only four miles from the centre of Nottingham.

Steeped in history and mentioned in the Domesday Book it has many associations with royalty and according to the 'York City Records', Richard III was hunting at his lodge at 'Beskwood' when he was told of the approach of his enemy and rival Henry Tudor, who, after defeating Richard at Bosworth Field in 1485 brought to power the Tudor dynasty.

In 1683 it was bestowed by Charles II to his illegitimate son by Nell Gwynn, Henry Beauclerk, whom he created First Duke of St. Albans. This first Duke was Registrar of the High Court of Chancery and Master Falconer of England.

Bestwood Lodge as we now know it was built by the 10th Duke of St. Albans in 1858, and completed in 1865 with thirty-six bedrooms. King Edward VII and Queen Alexandra stayed there when it was the property of the Beauclerk family, in whose hands it remained until 1938.

The stories of ghosts concerning Bestwood Lodge Hotel and the surrounding parkland are legion, and as one negotiates the twisting tree lined drive after dark and the gothic building is revealed in ones headlights it is not difficult to understand why.

To my mind the best time to visit it is on a cold winter's night, as the Foyer Bar with its blazing log fire reflected in the oak panelling seems to encourage you to sit by the huge stone hearth and consider the many ghost tales associated with the hotel.

A colleague of mine told me of his grandmother's experience when engaged there in a domestic capacity during the 1930's. She had occasion to go down to the cellars where she saw the misty figure of a woman in a long grey dress walk down a flight of steps and on reaching the bottom, the phantom slowly fade away.

This experience so unnerved her that she promptly gave notice even though jobs at that time were scarce.

The present owner Mr. John Lowe very kindly showed me round these cellars which, according to my informant, were quite extensive at the time of the incident. Today many are bricked up as a result of considerable renovation.

A former waitress at the hotel claims to have encountered a similar figure quite recently in the bar which in bygone days was the chapel. Again it was a woman in grey which as before slowly disappeared.

Suspended high above the Foyer Bar is a huge chandelier, and on more than one occasion after the doors are locked and glasses washed, barstaff have sat chatting and observed this chandelier slowly swinging to and fro as if pushed by invisible hands.

A check of the windows revealed that none were open, and if that were so, it would take more than a breeze to move the chandelier due to its considerable weight.

Local people aver that it is the ghost of Nell Gwynn which roams the hotel and parkland. It is of interest to note that occasionally certain areas of the hotel are pervaded by the faint aroma of oranges. Nell Gwynn was an orange seller before becoming an actress and attracting the attention of the King.

A lady in West Bridgford informed me of the experience of her brother and a friend who were walking through Bestwood Park just before the last war. Darkness was just beginning to settle when they heard a horse galloping along the path towards them, but nothing was to be seen. The hoofbeats became louder and closer and the two men stood rooted to the spot with fear, unable to move as the invisible animal bore down on them. Just when it seemed that it would crash into them they threw themselves backwards, the hoofbeats receding into the distance. Both men claim that they heard the rattle of bridle and bit over the drumming of hooves as it hurtled by.

A retired miner who worked at Bestwood Colliery claims to have seen a lady in white on several occasions in the park

Bestwood Lodge Hotel

when on his way to work for the night shift. Then in 1974 a party of Scouts camping in the park were terrified when they too saw a similar figure.

Shortly after this incident two youths arrived home in a state of panic one night after taking a short cut through the park. They insist that they were followed for over a mile by white wraith-like figures which kept to the trees.

Until recently an acquaintance of mine lived in Bestwood village and each day would take his Alsatian dog for a walk in the park. On reaching a certain area the animal's hackles would rise, and it would emit pitiful whines and howls, trying to pull away with its tail between its legs. On several occasions he tried to coax the animal to enter this area and each time it reacted in the same distressed manner. It is well known that animals are far more sensitive than humans in their awareness of the paranormal, and the dog's reaction would seem to indicate phenomena at this spot. In view of the stories recorded here it is highly likely.

These then, are but a few of the many strange tales from Bestwood Lodge. I cannot explain why this pleasant hotel and parkland should abound with so many varied reports. When considering its associations and their antiquity, then lost somewhere in the obscurity of the past must lie the answer.

Newstead Abbey

Every year, thousands of visitors flock to Newstead Abbey which is, of course, famous for its association with the poet Lord Byron, and contains many mementoes of his life. On a hot summer's day it is very pleasant to stroll in its superb grounds and gardens, but a visit by night, when the mist swirls in from the lake, presents a very different and eerie picture.

Newstead Abbey

The Abbey and grounds are reputed to be haunted by several ghosts, the best known being that of the Black Friar, whose origins go back to the days when the Abbey was a Priory belonging to the Augustinians or Black Canons. Its appearance is said to herald bad luck for anyone who meets it. Byron, with wry humour, claimed to have encountered it shortly before his ill-fated marriage to Ann Millbanke.

I know of only three sightings in recent years. One is supposedly by a doctor who, having recently moved into the Ravenshead area, was called out one night to visit a patient, but subsequently lost his way. He saw a figure standing by the main gates wearing a black duffel coat with the hood up, but closer observation revealed it to be wearing a monk's habit. The figure then disappeared. The doctor drove off rapidly.

Unfortunately, I can find no evidence to support this story, and although I have heard it from several people, no-one seems to know when it occurred, or the doctor's name, so I think we have to consider it to be apocryphal.

Then came a report from a poacher who saw my advertisement for ghost stories in the local paper. He telephoned me to say that he had used parts of the Abbey grounds for many years and was well aware of the tales associated with it but had never seen anything of a ghostly nature himself. That is, until late one night in June 1984, when going about his 'business' on the far side of the lake he claimed that he saw a figure walking toward him clad in a black duffel coat.

Slipping behind a nearby bush he realised he could not hear footsteps and, as it came closer, he saw it was not a duffel coat the figure was wearing but a monk's habit. As it passed by him, the cool night air became icy cold. The figure carried on walking for a few yards and then vanished.

Poachers are not over-imaginative as the nature of their 'occupation' would not allow for this. After a lengthy telephone conversation with this gentleman, I formed the impression that his report was quite genuine but, unfortunately, he declined to grant me an interview which, when considering the circumstances of his encounter, is perhaps understandable.

Another recent report comes from one of the Abbey staff. This gentleman had worked there for many years and had never experienced anything untoward. But late one afternoon when down in the crypt he saw a monk which promptly disappeared.

The White Lady Restaurant which is situated in a wing of the Abbey is named after another ghost which roams the area. This is thought to be the shade of Sophia Hyatt, who lived in the Abbey grounds at Weir Mill Farm and was killed in a coaching accident by the Abbey main gate. Some reports state that the accident occurred in Nottingham.

An interesting story came from a lady when walking along a

lonely lane on the Northern side of Newstead Park in the early 1900's. It was raining heavily and dusk was turning into darkness when she heard a low moaning in the wind which seemed to be mingled with the sound of human voices. As the sound grew nearer she saw in the dwindling light, two figures on horseback. One was a man clad entirely in black, the other a woman attired from head to foot in white. Neither appeared to notice the lady, nor seemed to be affected by the rain. The lady could not see their faces as they rode by, or hear the drumming of the horses' hooves; all she heard was the low moaning in the wind which accompanied them on their way.

On taking a half curious, half fearful, backwards look at the riders, she saw them fade into one of the parkside hedges. She then resolved to see if her imagination had been playing tricks by examining the hedge at the spot where the riders had gone through, but there was no sign of disturbance. She then examined the muddy path over which they had ridden but it showed no evidence of horses' hooves.

What then had the lady seen? Was it imagination? Had the years slipped away and had she witnessed the shade of Byron and his only true love, his half sister, Augusta Leigh?

The ghost of Sir John Byron has been encountered in the library at Newstead Abbey, sitting beneath his portrait as if to confirm his identity. His supposed mortal remains, together with his wife's, may lie in the crypt in the ornate tomb which was brought from their original resting place in Colwick Church.

Other ghosts at the Abbey include Byron's dog Boatswain, whose remains lie near a monument in the grounds and to whom Byron penned the monument's poignant inscription.

The cloisters are said to be the lurking place of a shapeless black mass with glowing eyes, but perhaps the strangest apparition of all is a column of white vapour which is alleged to rise out of the floor in one of the panelled bedrooms.

But now let us return to more recent reports of the paranormal at Newstead Abbey.

A young lady who helps out there during the summer claims that she was touched by an invisible 'something' when down in the crypt, and an electrician when working in the oratory next to Byron's bedroom swears that there was a presence in the room with him.

Mrs. Price, who shares the post of caretaker with her husband, told me that one day when dusting around the fireplace in Byron's bedroom, she became aware of a feeling that she was not alone and, as this realisation grew, she heard the sound of laboured breathing by her side. She admitted that the incident shook her so much that it was two days before she regained her nerve and returned. She assured me that she had never experienced anything of this nature before, even though she visits the room regularly.

For the serious 'ghost hunter', the invitation to spend some time in Newstead Abbey is a privilege indeed and this invitation was generously extended to the Nottingham Psychical Research Group by the Nottingham City Council with the kind co-operation of Mr. and Mrs. Price.

How would the reader feel, after musing on the strange and eerie tales, at being left alone in Newstead Abbey after dark, when the last tourist had departed and silence reigned again over the ancient building?

After some thought it was decided that we should confine our investigations to the crypt, oratory and Byron's bedroom, these being the locations where the most recent phenomena had occurred.

Jack Lumsden and myself decided to occupy Byron's room in comparative comfort, whilst Roy Westerman and Bob Sisson would 'enjoy' the discomfort of the unfurnished oratory next door.

Sitting in the silence of Byron's room amid a selection of the poet's personal possessions, a sense of the past becomes very real. There is his gilt four-poster bedstead which he used when at Trinity College, Cambridge, and on the walls a selection of prints, together with a Chippendale style mirror above the fireplace, to list but a few.

The oratory on the other hand, is a bleak and forbidding chamber with bare stone walls and a heavily-beamed ceiling, its gloom relieved only by the three leaded windows.

During our vigil, Jack and I went downstairs to the crypt in order to set up some equipment. This is a cavernous vault which echoed to our footsteps as we placed our equipment. It is dominated by the huge ornate tomb of Sir John Byron and his wife, their likenesses preserved by the two painted figures which repose with their hands clasped in prayer. Both Jack and I felt in more ways than one that the dead were not far away.

Unfortunately, our stay at Newstead Abbey passed all too quickly and phantoms did not honour us with their presence, nor did the equipment we had placed at various points show any sudden drops in temperature, or the recorders play back any disembodied voices. This, of course means nothing. Anyone who has seriously investigated the paranormal will agree that ghosts do not appear to order.

Rufford Abbey

Encompassed by a magnificent country park which opened to the public in 1970, stand the remains of the once proud Rufford Abbey, built by the monastic order of Cistercians and long regarded as being haunted. Following the dissolution of the abbey by Henry VIII in 1536, it became the home of the powerful Talbot family in whose hands it remained until 1626, when the estate passed to Sir George Savile of Yorkshire, whose decendants continued to live at Rufford until 1938.

Rufford Abbey

Today Rufford Abbey is being restored to something of its former grandeur by the Ancient Monuments Branch of the Department of the Environment and a section of the West Front is currently occupied.

Ghosts and legends abound. at Rufford and one may encounter not only a traditional 'White Lady' in the ruins, or gliding through the trees, but also 'The Little Old Lady in Black' on her perambulations through the park.

An obscure legend has it that many years ago a child was pursued through the corridors of Rufford and whilst frantically trying to hide in one of the massive four poster beds was caught and murdered. This legend in common with many others, has no doubt a basis in fact.

Over the years when Rufford was the home of the Saviles, several guests have awoken to the disconcerting experience of feeling a small shivering child nestling up to them as if for comfort and safety. On each occasion, a search revealed nothing.

A far more sinister ghost than this pathetic echo of the past is the Rufford 'Black Friar', a gigantic figure with a death's head under its cowl. This had a penchant for being seen reflected in mirrors and for tapping people on the shoulder. There are very few genuine records of anyone actually dying of fright as the result of an encounter with a ghost but the Edwinstowe church burial register tells how a local man died after meeting the 'Black Friar' in the 1900's.

When unsafe parts of Rufford Abbey were being demolished in the 1950's many of the ex-servants were genuinely worried that the disturbance might cause a renewed outbreak of hauntings, especially by the 'White Lady' which they had encountered many times. Their feelings that 'ghosts should be left well alone' is a sentiment no doubt endorsed by many.

Sherwood Manor

For many years there have been reports of a figure in a frock coat and top hat haunting the Sherwood Manor, formerly the Garden City Hotel on Mansfield Road, Sherwood, Nottingham. It has been seen in various parts of the building but usually in the cellar, where it has been encountered by deliverymen from the brewery on several occasions. It is thought to be the ghost of a former owner of the building when it was a private residence in the Victorian era.

A colleague of mine worked at the Sherwood Manor when it was the Garden City Hotel and told me that it was quite common to re-enter the cellar shortly after neatly stacking the beer crates only to discover them strewn around the floor. He had himself seen a dark figure down there from time to time.

Sherwood Manor

'Duke of Wellington' Kirkby in Ashfield

Extended and refurbished in recent years 'The Duke' is thought to be the oldest public house in Kirkby-in-Ashfield. Periodically, pets at the premises become very restless in the small hours. On more than one occasion successive licensees have entered the bar in the morning to discover tables and chairs overturned or piled in a heap, hearing nothing of the disturbance during the night. The bar is situated in the oldest part of the building.

These mysterious happenings are thought to have some connection with a sealed off tunnel in the cellar below the bar, which is said to lead to the nearby church of St. Wilfrid's and the neighbouring vicarage.

Duke of Wellington

'Trip to Jerusalem' - Nottingham

Of Nottingham's medieval castle, well known to thousands as the stronghold of the legendary Robin Hood's arch enemy, the Sheriff of Nottingham, little now remains but the restored gatehouse and some recently excavated foundations. Erected by order of William the Conqueror in 1068, the castle had a very turbulent career.

During the reign of King Stephen 1135-1154, it was destroyed and rebuilt on two occasions. During a Welsh rebellion, King John hanged twenty-eight hostages from its walls. In 1651 during the Civil War, it was pulled down by Parliamentarians and from 1674-9 it was rebuilt as we know it today, in the style of a baroque mansion by the Duke of Newcastle. Gutted by fire in 1831 by an angry mob in reaction to the Reform Bill, it remained a ruin until 1875 when it was restored by the Nottingham Corporation to serve as the city's art gallery and museum.

Trip To Jerusalem

The 'Trip to Jerusalem', however, which nestles under the Castle Rock is thought to be the original brewhouse for the castle and a sign on the wall declares it to be the oldest inn in England, AD 1189. It was here in the reign of King Richard I that the crusaders would stop for food and drink on their way to the Holy Land to fight for the cross and 'trypp' is the old-English word for 'halt'.

The 'Trip' is a fascinating inn with many curios adorning its bars. Together with the cellars, it is cut into the Castle Rock and is connected by numerous tunnels to a labyrinth of caves beneath the castle. Prior to the last War, there were many reports of ghostly noises echoing through the subterranean regions of the inn. One night during the War, some American servicemen were leaving the inn, when they heard a woman's voice screaming from above them 'Bel fitz, eiez pitie du gentil Mortimer'!

To look for an explanation for this phrase it is necessary to consider the events which occured on the night of October 19, 1330, during the reign of Edward III, when Roger Mortimer, Earl of March, (lover of Queen Isabella, the widow of murdered Edward II and mother of Edward III) occupied the castle. On Edward's orders, a party of conspirators came to the 'Trip to Jerusalem' and entered the castle by a secret tunnel (since known as Mortimer's Hole). They were met by Edward and taken to his mothers room. Led by Edward, the conspirators burst in and the King himself seized Mortimer, ignoring his mother's entreaty: "Bel fitz, eiez pitie du gentil Mortimer!" — "Fair son, have pity on the gentle Mortimer!"

Mortimer was then placed in a dungeon before being taken to London, accused of usurping the King's authority and to having 'murdered and killed the King's father'. On 29th November he was dragged on a hurdle from the Tower to be hung, drawn and quartered at Tyburn.

The Park, Nottingham

The setting for this story is an area in Nottingham called the Park, which is a village within the city, built to provide select and restful seclusion for the lace factory owners and other wealthy citizens.

It was told to me by a lady from Wollaton, now a very lucid seventy-eight year old, who came with her parents from London to live in The Park when she was fifteen. Shortly after the family had settled in, she was invited by neighbours, with whom her parents had become acquainted, to their son's birthday party.

When she arrived at their house it was over-run by children and, after a feast of cakes, ice-cream and jelly, they played various party games. Someone suggested playing hide-and-seek, and she was nominated to be 'it'. She was given a count of one hundred to start and, as the counting began, she ran upstairs to find a suitable hiding place.

After considering two bedrooms and rejecting them as too obvious, she ran down a short corridor and slipped inside a small room through its partly open door.

This room, unlike the rest of the house, was neither decorated nor furnished and had a strange, forbidding atmosphere. As she stood with her back to the door she heard someone sobbing and saw, huddled in a corner, a little girl in an odd sort of costume. She was about to ask her what was wrong and why she wasn't downstairs with the others when she slowly faded away. Puzzled but not alarmed by this, she returned downstairs to find the owners of the house and, as she explained what had happened, they exchanged worried glances. When she had finished, the lady of the house said that due to the excitement of the party, she must have imagined the whole thing but made her promise not to tell the other children about it.

Many years later, she learned that the house was haunted and that that particular room was normally kept locked. She never learned the story behind the haunting and perhaps now we never will, for the house was demolished some years ago.

But in an area such as The Park, redolent with memories of nannies, servants and cooks, there must be many stories such as this which still remain to be told.

Mapperley Park, Nottingham

Mapperley Park has many large Victorian houses, legacies of the wealthy owners of the lace factories and other successful entrepreneurs. Today many have been converted into flats and it was in one such house on Redcliffe Road that 'Jane Smith' rented a top floor flat in 1975.

The flat had been unoccupied for some time previously and was in need of redecoration. The pressure of a demanding job at the Queen's Medical Centre deemed that she defer the task for a while. Shortly after moving in, Jane sensed that all was not as it should be in her new home. It was nothing she could explain, just an indefinable something in the atmosphere. Then one night, as she was preparing for bed, she became aware that the atmosphere in the flat was considerably more oppressive than usual, but it had been a long day and she was soon abed in a deep sleep.

It seemed that she had not been asleep for long before she woke and found that the atmosphere in the room had undergone a subtle change. It felt as if it were charged with a feeling of expectancy. As her eyes became accustomed to the darkness, she saw, standing in the middle of the room, an elderly woman wearing a long grey dress. Jane felt a baleful aura radiating from the figure which then disappeared. Switching on the bedside light, Jane sought to convince herself that it must have been her imagination. Was it due to the effect of a demanding job and recent personal problems?

Nothing further occurred until several months later, when as before, she awoke in the small hours to find the woman in grey. This time the figure did not disappear, and Jane was horrified to see it advance slowly towards her with its hands outstretched and with an expression of malignancy on its aged features.

Slowly, the figure came closer and the feeling of evil in the room became almost palpable. Jane found herself unable to move or cry out as it advanced. With eyes full of hate, the figure slowly placed its icy hands around her neck and began to squeeze. Inexplicably Jane did not experience the expected sense of being choked but of suffocation and with this realisation, something enabled her to reach out and switch the light on. At this the figure released its grip, backed off and slowly faded away.

For the remainder of the night Jane dozed in an armchair in the sitting room with the lights on and, as dawn broke, she was resolved to look for another flat.

The weeks turned to months, and the figure did not reappear. By now she had a steady relationship with Chris, who moved into the flat with her. Due to a combined effort the flat was completely redecorated.

Jane awoke one night, to see the woman in grey standing by the bedroom window. This time her intuition told her that it meant her no harm and she awoke Chris. When he looked, the figure had gone.

A few months later the couple decided to marry and began house-hunting. Finding a suitable property she gave the landlord notice for vacating the flat. By coincidence, Bill and Mary in a flat across the corridor were also leaving and invited Jane and Chris for drinks as a celebration. Towards the end of the evening, Bill remarked that he would be interested if the new tenants of his flat experienced anything strange after they had moved in. Jane asked him what he meant by this. He related how both Mary and he had, on several occasions, seen the ghost of an old woman in a long grey dress in the flat and corridor. He felt that she was waiting for an opportunity to harm them in some way but, as neither were ever alone in the flat, the opportunity never arose. But the strange thing was as they got the flat decorated and generally straightened out the figure appeared less frequently and had not been seen for over two years. He never mentioned the ghost to the landlord but learned from one of the tenants that the top floor which now comprised the two flats was, in the old days, the servants' quarters.

Forest Road, Nottingham

Secret rooms feature in many ghost stories and one such room existed at a Georgian house overlooking the Forest Recreation Ground on Forest Road East.

Following the demise of the last occupants the building fell into a semi-derelict condition and due to the attention of vandals it became necessary to board up the doors and ground floor windows.

A strange story was told to me about this house, concerning two decorators who shortly after the last war, had been engaged to redecorate throughout.

Having stripped the paper from the upper rooms the men proceeded to start on one of the hallways and on what appeared to be a solid wall. Imagine their surprise when they discovered a door sealed round with lead underneath the paper.

Mystified and intrigued at their find the two men decided to open the door, by peeling away the lead. They managed with some difficulty. According to one of them, it was as if they had opened the door of a deep freeze unit, so intense was the coldness. They glimpsed a flight of stairs curving upwards into the darkness, then 'something' they could not see, physically forced them backwards away from the opening. Throwing down their tools they fled from the house. One of them later telephoned the owner to say that they would not be back to finish the decorating.

A few days after hearing this story I went along with my wife to see the house for myself. It certainly looked mysterious standing behind its black iron gates with the overgrown garden lying under a carpet of decaying leaves. At the back of the house we found one window which had had the boards forced away, and by peering into the darkness we could barely see a large panelled room with a fireplace at one end. Unfortunately, I had neglected to bring a torch with me so we did not venture inside, but at least we'd found a way in with a view to spending a night on the premises.

As we were leaving, we saw four young ladies walking down the driveway of one of the houses nearby. Wondering if they might know of any local stories concerning the house, we caught up with them and I explained why I was interested in the house.

One of the young ladies lived nearby and both she and her parents were familiar with the story of the decorators, having heard it from the former occupants.

She told us that the room had been sealed previously at the insistence of a maid at the house, who flatly refused to carry on working there if it were not. She did not know why it had been sealed with lead. Furthermore she seemed to remember having heard that that part of the house in which the room was situated was once used as a nursery, and the cellars were said to lead to the cemetery on Mansfield Road, nearby. This is likely as Nottingham is honeycombed with caves, and there are catacombs leading from this cemetery.

She also told us that shortly after the last occupant died, a fire had gutted the central part of the house but no cause could be found to account for it. It was attributed to a vagrant who might have broken in to seek a nights shelter, but this was only a supposition.

The following Saturday evening, having first informed the local police, three members of the Chesterfield Psychical Research Society (now sadly disbanded) Jack Lumsden and myself were making our way down the tree lined drive of the house. It certainly presented a dismal and eerie aspect by night. We entered by the window at the rear, and went in search of the secret room discovered by the decorators.

Inside, the house was like a warren, with long corridors and curving passageways, the beams of our torches causing shadows to dance weirdly on the walls around us.

On reaching the central part of the house we came across the area damaged by the fire and we all agreed that it had a disquieting atmosphere with its blistered panelling and charred staircase, especially with the night breeze rattling the corrugated iron which had been placed over the gaping windows.

Moving yet deeper into the house we eventually found a doorway set flush into a wall. By shining our torches we saw steps curving upwards into the darkness. This fitted the description given by the decorators, and although the door had gone, the entrance did show signs of being sealed.

Slowly, in single file, we made our way up the narrow staircase and rounding a corner discovered a door at the top. On pressing down the latch the door swung slowly inwards, revealing to our torchbeams a small windowless L-shaped room with a ceiling so low we had to stoop as we went inside. A person of average size could not be comfortable in a room with such a low ceiling, but we discovered the walls to be papered indicating that it had once been occupied. We also discovered that the door at the top of the stairs had some large nails, long since rusted, driven into the frame at the point where the door would latch and the remains of some wire which appeared to have been used to keep the door shut, although strangely, we found no trace of a lock or bolt.

As it was totally impractical for five people to spend a night in the room we left a cassette recorder, and after sealing the door with tape went downstairs to examine the area around the room. It is of interest to note that architecturally there was no evidence inside the house or out to suggest that such a room existed.

Back in the comparative comfort of the panelled room, we returned upstairs to change the cassette tapes and re-seal the door to the secret room. At approximately 4.00am we discovered that the tape that we had placed over the door was on the floor. We then retrieved the cassette player and played it back but it revealed nothing but our footsteps descending the stairs. Once more we went upstairs and placed a new recorder in the room and re-sealed the door and kept watch outside. After a suitable time had elapsed we peeled away the tape and played back the recorder which as before revealed nothing. The remainder of the night passed without incident and we departed at dawn leaving the mystery of the house and its concealed room to its secrets.

If walls could talk what could this house reveal of a past and events that deemed it necessary to seal off one of its rooms with lead.

Bonington House now a Labour Party Club, Arnold

Ask anyone in Arnold what they can tell you of the imposing Georgian house in the High Street and they will readily point out that it is Bonington House, birthplace of the celebrated artist, Richard Parkes Bonington, and now the Arnold Labour Party Club.

What is less well known, is that it appears to harbour a ghost.

A previous stewardess of the club, told me that shortly after taking up the post, she and her husband became aware that certain rooms on the second floor had, at times, a rather unpleasant atmosphere and would suddenly turn icy cold for no apparent reason.

In the domestic quarters, small articles such as keys would go missing and then turn up several days later. Inexplicable noises were heard in the small hours, which to pacify their growing disquiet, they attributed to the age of the building.

However, in spite of this reasoning, their fear that they were not the only occupants of the building was confirmed in such a manner that caused the stewardess to have to undergo medical treatment for severe shock.

Shortly before opening time one evening, she went to the bathroom and on opening the door she saw to her horror, a figure glide slowly into the room through the wall. It was attired in a broad brimmed hat and a long dark cloak. This was all the detail she ascertained before fear got the upper hand. She fled downstairs.

Thoroughly shaken, the couple got in touch with the previous tenants who confirmed that they too had seen the figure on a number of occasions.

These events happened many years ago and the present committee inform me that whilst they had seen nothing of a ghostly nature, strange things still happen from time to time; beer taps in the cellar suddenly switch off and on investigation technical faults cannot be found, lights had been discovered to be switched on in the mornings which were switched off the night before. Pranksters can be ruled out as the building has an efficient intruder alarm system, connected to the local police station.

The upper storeys of the building where the stewardess saw the figure which gave her such a fright, are now seldom used, apart from the rooms used by a local diving club. A modern extension at the rear of the building fulfils the principal purpose of the club.

Arnold Labour Party Club

It is interesting to speculate on the reasons why the club would seem to be haunted. There are no lurid tales of murder or suicide connected with the building. In the main such tales give rise to such a reputation.

Could it be that, when the last revellers have gone home, and the building is secured for the night, the shade of Parkes

Bonington himself roams his birthplace? Was the building in years gone by the scene of crime and tragedy that has never been recorded?

The next time you pass by or visit the Arnold Labour Party Club, pause and reflect on this, and remember, it is not only one of the oldest buildings in Arnold, it is also the most enigmatic — and long may it remain so.

Newdigate House
The French Connection

In February 1705 the great soldier-statesman, the Duc de Tallard, arrived in Nottingham following his defeat by the Duke of Marlborough at the Battle of Blenheim in 1704.

Newdigate House

His captivity, although the term is hardly appropriate, was spent at Newdigate House in Castle Gate. Here he remained until 1712, when, much to the regret of many people, for he had become a popular figure, he returned to France.

Succesive occupants of Newdigate House have asserted that in the quiet hours just before dawn, they have been awakened by voices jesting in French and the click of billiard balls accompanied by strange music.

Slow measured footsteps have also been heard which pass down the hall and stop at the entrance to the oldest part of the house. They then change course to go through the original doorway, after which they fade away.

Marshall Tallard always maintained he would return to Nottingham and to his 'prison' at Newdigate House, but never did . . . . not in mortal form anyway.

Sherwood, Nottingham

As this story was recounted to me in a quiet and factual manner by a gentleman I have known for a number of years, I have no reason to doubt its authenticity. As it happened many years ago, I have no means of verifying the details with the people concerned.

The building he referred to was a large victorian house in the Sherwood area of Nottingham. When purchased by its new owners, it required a considerable amount of decorating and modernisation. After decorating the ground and upper floor, they decided to make a start on the bedrooms in the attic. They found that the door to the end bedrooms would not open, although they had not encountered any difficulties previously. Eventually, they forced the door and on examining it, they could find no reason to account for any difficulty.

Dismissing this of little consequence, they set to and papered the walls. Having completed this task some hours later, they retired for the night.

Equipped with paint and brushes they prepared to complete the room on the following day but once again had great difficulty opening the door. When they did manage to force it, they discovered the new wallpaper lying on the floor in sheets as if it had been peeled off. Assuming that they might somehow have mixed the paste incorrectly, they re-papered the walls. After planing the bottom of the door, so as to eliminate the problem of it jamming once and for all, they gave it a layer of undercoat.

The morning after, in spite of planing the door, they still had great difficulty gaining access to the room and once again they had to use considerable force to open it. On doing so, they found to their consternation that the wallpaper had again peeled onto the floor, but this time it had been shredded and was scattered around the room. Closer examination revealed that the original wallpaper which had been papered over was undamaged. Stranger still was the sight of the newly painted door. It looked as if someone had rubbed their hands in the paint and smeared it from the top to the bottom.

Leaving the room exactly as it was they put a padlock on the door and never ventured inside again.

Furlong Street, Arnold

Some years ago a terraced house on Furlong Street, Arnold, was the scene of considerable poltergeist activity, which, according to the occupants, rendered the property untenantable.

The haunting became so intolerable, that the occupants had to sleep in their car on several occasions. A medium was called in and this alleviated the problem for a time but the activity returned with renewed ferocity.

Taking the only course left open to them the occupants moved out.

There were rumours of a suicide at the house many years ago which could account for the haunting. This has never been substantiated.

Farmhouse at Stoke Bardolph

By the side of the River Trent, in the village of Stoke Bardolph, is an ancient farmhouse, which in 1982 was undergoing renovation by a team of builders. When the men began work on one of the attic landings they experienced a feeling of 'being watched'. Looking up from their work, they were surprised to see, at the end of a landing, an old lady holding a cat. She was observing them intently. They were even more surprised and not a little alarmed, when together with her pet, she disappeared. This, I was told, had occurred on several occasions on this particular landing. The old lady had not been encountered in any other part of the house.

Shortly after this story had been related to me, I visited the farmhouse. After leaving, I asked a gentleman who lives nearby, if he could tell me anything about the farm and, in particular, its previous owners. He informed me that the former owners had lived there for as long as he could remember. After the death of the farmer, his wife had gradually closed the farm down, and eventually she sold it to the Severn-Trent Water Authority. She moved into a house in the village where she died shortly afterwards. The authorities then decided to demolish the farmhouse but, having a change of heart, put a preservation order on the old building instead.

After standing empty for some years, it was purchased by the present owner, who set about its renovation. That, he said, was all he could tell me, but as an afterthought he remembered that the old lady was very fond of cats and after the death of her husband she had adopted several strays over the ensuing years.

This information was of interest, in view of the builders' story that the lady was always seen to be holding a cat. I told the gentleman why I was making enquiries about the property, and whilst he expressed great interest he could give no further information. He did suggest that I visit one of the farm workers, who, although long since retired, kept an eye on the farm, as its land adjoined his garden. I visited this gentleman and he confirmed that he had heard of the ghostly lady, and her pet, but had not encountered them himself.

Linda's Story

It is a sad thought, especially from an investigator's point of view, that over the years there must have been a multitude of buildings demolished which had an unrecorded story of a haunting associated with them. Thanks to Linda Mills of The Wells Road, Mapperley, one such story can now be told.

In 1960, when she was ten years of age, Linda, her parents, and her sister, moved into a victorian terraced house in Stapleford. Shortly after moving in, there came the first intimation of something 'odd' about the house. Pictures would regularly fall off the walls whenever anyone walked by them, but on examination the cords were always found to be intact. These minor irritants were largely ignored as the two girls and their father had more important things to concern them. For some time, the health of Linda's mother had been failing such that she could no longer walk, and had become bed-ridden. It then became necessary for her to occupy the sitting room downstairs.

It was shortly after her mother had moved into this room that Linda became aware, whilst sometimes chatting with her mother, of a presence in the room. On several occasions they heard stertorous breathing. Whenever Linda mentioned this, her mother admonished her for imagining the presence, the breathing noise she was told, was due to old houses making strange noises and that it was nothing for her to worry about.

Linda became convinced that the house was haunted when her sister, a few years older than herself, began to go out in the evenings. When Linda had gone to bed and her father had been up to say goodnight, he would make sure his wife was comfortable downstairs and then go across the road to a club. This meant that there was only Linda and her mother left in the house.

Times without number, after Linda's father had left the house and whilst reading in bed, she would hear the stair door open. Footsteps would ascend the stairs, and proceed along the landing to stop outside her bedroom door. The door would then slowly open, and after a pause of several seconds, would close. She would again hear the footsteps retreat along the landing, descend the stairs and hear the stair door open and close.

Due to the position of her bed, Linda could not see what was behind her bedroom door when it opened, although she often wondered. Wondered, but never dared leave her bed to find out.

In the late 1960's, this house was condemned to the demolition man's hammer. It was not until the family were settled in their new home that Linda learnt that the house had indeed been haunted. On questioning her parents they both admitted that they too had experienced inexplicable happenings but had made light of them so as not to cause alarm to their two daughters. They had since learnt from neighbours that the house was reputed to have been haunted by an old lady who had committed suicide there many years previously by gassing herself.

New Lenton

Perhaps the most bizarre account of a haunting in Nottinghamshire was related to me by a friend of my wife's. To preserve her anonymity, I will call her Barbara.

Barbara worked at an office with a young lady who, together with her parents and brother, had moved recently into a large old house on Arundel Street, which lies between Derby Road and Ilkeston Road, New Lenton in Nottingham. Shortly after, they realised that the house was haunted. Occasionally when they were watching television the lounge door would slowly open and their dog would become agitated. The dog's eyes would follow something approach the sofa which would then depress as if someone had sat on it. The family were not unduly worried by the thought of sharing their home with an unseen presence and adopted a policy of 'live and let live' towards it. After a while however, trivial but annoying incidents began to occur, such as when they came downstairs in the mornings, pictures would be found awry on the walls and ornaments would have been moved.

The ghost began to indicate more sinister traits when, on several occasions, the gas taps on the oven were found to be turned on. No one had seen the ghost until one night when the young lady's brother was awakened by the feeling of someone blowing on his neck. He saw, standing by his bed, a shadowy figure dressed in the manner of an 'old fashioned coachman'. This then vanished.

A few weeks later, the young lady's brother-in-law was also roused in the night by someone prodding him in the back. He could not see anyone in the room but on going onto the landing, he too saw a shadowy figure in strange garb. This also faded away.

It was decided to make contact with the previous occupants of the property, to see if they could offer some explanation which might account for the haunting. They discovered that the last people to live there had been two old ladies, but one had recently died and the other, now in her late eighties, was in a nursing home and was senile. They learnt nothing of any value from her.

One day the young lady invited Barbara and some friends from the office to her home for lunch and afterwards took them on a tour of the house.

They began with the attics which were as yet undecorated and empty, save for an old rocking chair which the previous occupants had left behind. Everyone in the party remarked on the air of disquiet in these attics. The young lady pointed to something ominous — a mark which appeared to be a dried bloodstain on the floorboards. She said that no amount of scrubbing would remove it.

Shortly afterwards, whilst sitting in the kitchen, Barbara felt very cold and sensed that something was in the room with them. She moved and sat by the window in the sunlight but she remained cold. She mentioned this to the others and everyone agreed that when considering the warmth of the sunny day, the kitchen had turned inordinately cold. At which point they decided to return to work.

When the young lady returned home that evening, she went to her room where, kicking off her shoes, she felt the carpet to be wet underfoot. Switching on the lights, she discovered that the carpet was spattered with blood, as were the bed and walls. She found the bathroom to be in a similar state, the bath towels looking as if someone had smeared their bloodied hands on them. In shock and terror she fled from the house and telephoned her parents from a nearby call box. On arrival her father found the rooms to be as his daughter had described and he telephoned for the police.

When the police arrived, their first thought was that the family had been the victim of a sick joke and examined the house thoroughly, paying particular attention to the doors and windows. They found nothing to indicate that the house had been broken into but, before leaving, they took some samples of blood with them for examination by the pathology laboratory.

The family reached the conclusion that the ghost resented their occupation. If it were capable of this, what might it do next in its endeavours to drive them out? They decided that the best course of action was to put the house up for sale immediately. The young lady and her brother would meanwhile go and stay with relatives.

When the police got in touch a few days later they were even more convinced that they had made the right decision. The tests had revealed that the blood had come from a corpse prior to rigor mortis having set in.

Shortly after hearing this story, I mentioned it to a policeman friend, who was stationed at the local police station at the time of the incident, and whilst he had no personal involvement, he would vouch for the authenticity of this event.

Calverton

In Main Street, Calverton is a charming seventeenth century cottage, the home of Mr. & Mrs. Cupitt. It was here, as we sat by the large inglenook fireplace, with the glow of the flames dancing on the heavily beamed ceiling, that Mrs. Eileen Cupitt, curator of the Calverton Folk Museum told me of the many ghosts which haunt this attractive village.

Mr. & Mrs. Cupitt came to view their cottage in 1947, which at that time was derelict and unprepossessing, with water streaming down the walls and a weed tangled garden. Mrs. Cupitt decided to take a look upstairs, and it was when she came down again that she felt a hand on her shoulder and heard a voice say 'buy this place. You will be happy here'. She realised that it was haunted.

Home of Mr. & Mrs. Cupitt, Calverton

Buy the cottage they did, and with much hard work transformed the derelict building into the delightful residence it is today. It was not until some three years after moving in that Mrs. Cupitt saw a ghost in her home.

Their young daughter, who usually slept soundly, became very restless one night. Mrs. Cupitt went upstairs to sit with her and as she lulled the little girl to sleep, she happened to glance up to see an elderly man wearing a gingery tweed jacket and knee breeches. He was staring with a sad expression out of the window when he disappeared.

It was by visiting one of Calvertons' oldest residents, Mr. John Davis who came to live there in 1902, that Mrs. Cupitt learnt more about the ghost. It transpired that Mr. Davis lived in their cottage many years before and he asked if she had ever seen the ghost. He then told her that he too had frequently seen the figure of an elderly man, wearing a tweed jacket, staring out of the bedroom window. He appeared to be watching the children on their way to school.

Some eighteen months after hearing this, Mrs. Cupitt was visited by the vicar of Calverton who she knew well. He asked her if she had ever experienced anything odd at her cottage and she told him of the ghost upstairs. The vicar then showed her a letter. It was from a lady in Australia who had written to him having heard that several cottages in Calverton had been demolished, asking if Mr. & Mrs. Cupitts' had been one of them. The letter went on to say that the cottage had once belonged to her great-great grandfather who had been the headmaster of the local school . . . . . . and was said to haunt the cottage.

Georges Hill

Overshadowed in parts by the branches of trees which reach out to form a gloomy tunnel over this winding lane, Georges Hill is shunned even today by many people after dark, as there are several well attested reports of a figure clad in black which haunts the area.

Georges Hill, Calverton

Mr. Lawrence Bardhill encountered this figure when returning from Nottingham's Goose Fair in the 1930's. He had reached the brow of Georges Hill and heard the village clock chime midnight, when as he passed a gateway 'something' came out of the shadows at his side. It wore a large hat under which he could not discern any features other than a large hooked nose. Round its neck hung a large silver chain, below this was nothing but an amorphous black mass.

Understandably Mr. Bardhill crossed to the other side of the road, but the figure followed him, moving with a strange gliding motion. He began to walk faster, then broke into a run, but effortlessly the figure kept pace with him and did so for nearly a quarter of a mile before leaving him by gliding into another gateway.

Mr. Bardhill continued his flight until he reached home, where he collapsed onto a sofa to be found by his brother-in-law the next morning. It was some time before Mr. Bardhill stopped shaking and was able to describe his unnerving experience lucidly, he was ill for several days afterwards.

Mr. Bardhill's encounter was frightening enough, but imagine how a lady felt when driving down Georges Hill one night quite recently, and saw, when glancing in her rear view mirror a black, hatted figure sitting in the back of her car. It stayed with her for several seconds before vanishing and the lady in her panic very nearly crashed the car. A young couple I know very well, saw a figure in black which fits the description of Mr. Bardhill's phantom when driving down Georges Hill one night in 1984.

Calverton Hall

Prior to its demolition in 1961, to make way for the miners' welfare, Calverton Hall was for many years used as the vicarage, and another place which many of the older residents of the village avoided after dark.

Many dogs refused to walk on the pavement alongside the building and one lady whose journey meant passing the Hall one night, waited nervously at a discreet distance until she could find someone to accompany her. Before long she saw a lady walking down the road and hurrying to catch up with her, she suddenly turned and faded into the wall of the Hall.

Mr. Dennis Cupitt had a similar experience one night when he approached a lady in the driveway of the Hall. At the rear of the building were some stables which had been converted into Scouts' Headquarters. He was locking up when he saw a lady nearby and greeted her thinking her to be the vicar's wife, but she disappeared.

Another strange report came from a bus driver who stopped to allow a lady to board late one night only to discover afterwards that she had unaccountably vanished when the conductor went to collect her fare.

Information has been provided by one resident which may account for the ghostly woman who roams this area. He recalls that in 1936, a skeleton with a hole in its skull, was discovered in the rose garden of Calverton Hall.

Calverton Hall was demolished by two men from London and as they found difficulty in finding lodgings locally were put up by Mr. & Mrs. Hoyle at the new vicarage. A few days after starting to demolish the Hall they arrived back at the vicarage earlier than usual and had a strange story to tell.

As they began to secure the building for the night they heard footsteps upstairs. One of the men went up the servants staircase and the other up the main staircase in order to trap whoever was there. Pausing by a door they could hear the footsteps pacing up and down. They flung open the door and found that thay had already removed the floorboards from that particular room. The footsteps continued. Suddenly there was a crashing noise as if someone were smashing china . . . . then total silence. The men fled.

Shortly after this incident it was discovered that in 1876 a maid at the Hall was to be married to a local coachman. Just before the wedding day he jilted her and the girl committed suicide in one of the bedrooms. Subsequently, generations of families at the hall had at some time or another claimed to have experienced feelings of sadness, heard inexplicable noises, and felt intense coldness in various rooms.

Calverton Folk Museum

On Main Street, Calverton is a stockingers cottage dating from 1780, which was derelict until a few years ago. Due to the endeavours of Mrs. Cupitt and a party of helpers, it now serves as the Calverton Folk Museum and contains a host of artifacts, many of which pertain to the framework knitting industry, for which Calverton was renowned for nearly three hundred years.

As the museum became established, the committee engaged the services of a local electrician, as the cottage lacked modern amenities. After examining the cottage the electrician concluded that the task would not take long and they left it in his hands. Time went and still the cottage was without electricity. Eventually the electrician was asked why he was taking such a long time with the job, to which he confessed that he did not like the atmosphere in the cottage and would only work there if accompanied. Accompanied he was, and the electricity was duly installed.

Interior of Calverton Folk Museum

A few months later Mrs. Cupitt was in the cottage one night together with four other people, sitting at a table cleaning and renovating various objects, when simultaneously they experienced an air of malevolence in the room. They leapt up from the table and hurriedly vacated the building. When Mrs. Cupitt returned later to switch off the lights the atmosphere had returned to normal. Several times since this incident Mrs. Cupitt has experienced this air of malevolence, and very often visitors to the museum have commented on it even in broad daylight. This, it seems is what the electrician had experienced and why he refused to work in there alone.

With the kind permission of Mrs. Cupitt the Nottingham Psychical Research Group were able to spend the night of Saturday 11th may 1985 at the Calverton Folk Museum. We began our vigil at 10.00pm and left at 4.30am as the first light of dawn appeared in the sky. Unfortunately the night passed without incident on this occasion but arrangements have been made for another stay in the near future.

These are but a few of the ghost stories to come from Calverton which must surely be the most haunted village in Nottinghamshire.

Forest Glade School
Sutton-in-Ashfield

Forest Glade, a victorian school at Sutton-in-Ashfield, now used for commercial purposes, was in 1985 haunted by the ghost of a little girl whose identity remains a mystery. Shortly after businessman Phillip Wishall and his mother, Lillian, set up a small textile factory in part of the school buildings, reports came from the staff of a 'presence'. Mrs. Wishall is in no doubt that she saw the blurred figure of a little girl who appeared to be wearing a duffel coat and wellington boots, whose age she estimated to be about seven years. Mr. Wishall also saw a similar figure and one member of the staff alleged that a figure spoke to her saying 'I don't want to go'.

Following the visit of a medium to the premises the sightings became less frequent, but mysterious happenings would still occasionally occur in the form of lights being switched on and off, cups moved from one place to another and papers moved around the building.

Shire Hall
High Pavement, Nottingham

Rebuilt in 1770 from the ruins of an older building which occupied the same site, Nottingham's Shire Hall on High Pavement houses the county's courts and legal offices. The justice administered there today is not as harsh as in the 'good old days', when many people paid for their crimes on the scaffold. This was erected on the steps in front of the building, (the removeable stone insets can still be seen today) and later, in the prison yard at the back.

Shire Hall

Many prisons and sites of execution are reputed to be haunted and the Shire Hall is no exception, although no details are known as to what or whom is alleged to stalk its ancient corridors and cells. Some people allude to stories of a ghostly female said to glide through brick walls, which are supposed to have been especially built in certain corridors to keep her at bay, but to no avail. Perhaps nearer the truth are reports from the cleaning staff, who whilst going about their work, tell of hearing doors slam and footsteps echoing in unoccupied regions of the building.

Reports such as these have persisted over many years at the Shire Hall and thanks to Mr. Brian Birchenall the building superintendant, it was arranged that Roy Westerman, Robert Sisson and myself would spend the night of Saturday 18th February 1984 in the old prison in order to investigate these.

Arriving at 7.00pm we were met by Mr. Birchenall who conducted us on a tour of the condemned cells and transportation cells, which even now, when brightly illuminated by electricity, present a gloomy aspect. It is not difficult to imagine the feelings of prisoners incarcerated there in bygone days with only rushlights or candles for comfort. A poignant reminder of those days are prisoners' names, which they carved on the walls whilst awaiting for their sentence to be carried out.

The exercise yard in particular evokes thoughts of those condemned to kick away their lives on the 'three-legged mare'. A replica of a gallows is displayed in the yard and many of the original's victims are interred beneath the flagstones.

I asked Mr. Birchenall if he had ever experienced anything unusual at the Shire Hall. Apart from the odd occasion in the antechamber of the cells, when he felt that there was someone there other than himself, he had not experienced anything he would care to call paranormal. He did mention however, that some of the residents of Cliff Road behind the building had occasionally claimed to have seen vague figures late at night at the exit for prisoners sentenced to transportation.

Mr. Birchenall departed at 7.30pm leaving us to make a leisurely exploration of the surroundings which we would occupy for the night. At 8.00pm we settled in the antechamber of the cells which are suitably adorned with chains and shackles. There we stayed until 9.30pm having decided to move into one of the principal transportation cells which are situated under the two condemned cells and reached by means of a step ladder.

We stayed in there until 11.30pm and then moved into the condemned cells, Roy occupying one cell, Bob and myself the other. By 12.30am nothing unusual had occurred, so a cassette recorder was left in each cell. We again descended the ladder into the transportation cells resolved to spend the rest of the night in there.

Time passed uneventfully until 4.55am when we saw in the adjacent chamber an oblong shape of light hovering about two feet above the floor. Switching on our torches caused it to disappear. We examined the area to see if we could find any indication as to its origin but found nothing which might account for it. Obviously being below ground with no windows or outside apertures, external light could not get into the chamber so this theory was immediately ruled out. After some thought the only explanation we could tentatively put forward was some form of freak reflection caused by the candle in our cell, but try as we might, by adjusting our chairs to different angles, we could not reproduce the effect.

We settled down again in the hope that it may reoccur, but unfortunately nothing further happened, and so at 6.00am we decided to leave. The subsequent playback of the cassette recorders left in the condemed cells revealed nothing of interest.

The Little London Herbal Stores Forman Street, Nottingham

In the nineteenth century, Nottingham, in common with many cities, had its quarters where, if it could be avoided, no respectable person would venture after dark. One in particular was North Street, then notorious as a red light area.

It was a place where drunken men brawled and gin sodden prostitutes in feathered hats leered hopefully at passers-by from the shelter of doorways, or stood under hissing gas lamps whose glow partially softened their prematurely aged features. It is very likely that they watched with appraising eyes the well dressed, middle-aged man, who appeared to be the epitome of respectability, taking a leisurely stroll through their tawdry domain on the night of 17th July 1884. For this gentleman was none other than Mr. Justice Charles Watkin Williams, one of Her Majesty's High Court Judges and that fateful stroll was to end in a death and a scandal which set tongues wagging for years afterwards, and gave Nottingham yet another ghost.

After leaving his lodgings in High Pavement, where he was staying whilst on one of his regular visits from London to the Nottingham Assizes, Sir Charles attempted to avail himself of the services provided by a prostitute. He called on Nellie Banks, at No. 23 North Street, a private house and brothel, where he suffered a fatal heart attack.

Due to the probity of Sir Charles' position, his body was taken back to his lodgings in an attempt to conceal the circumstances of his death. The truth, albeit for the most part speculative, became known and was the talk of the city.

Today, North Street is Forman Street and the house of ill-repute where Sir Charles expired is a well known shop, the 'Little London Herbal Stores'. The shadowy spectre of the judge is alleged to haunt a small, dusty room on the upper

The Little London Herbal Stores

floor, but has not been seen for many years. This room is now used as storage space.

The present owner of the premises Mr. Alan Freeman is well aware of the tales told about the ghostly judge but has never encountered it himself. But, when working late one winter's night, he heard a resounding crash in the room above and deciding he had done enough for one day, he quickly locked up and left. Perhaps that crash is an indication that the judges spirit still haunts the building.

A Club on Bridlesmith Gate Nottingham

Change or disturbance, usually structural alterations, very often seem to activate ghostly manifestations and related phenomena. The renovation of a club in Nottingham's Bridlesmith Gate in 1969, could be the reason for sporadic and eerie occurrences at these premises.

During the renovations, a basement room was discovered which was thought to be connected with the ancient network of caves upon which Bridlesmith Gate stands. Shortly afterwards and for some months following intermittent poltergeist activity occurred.

On several occasions members of the staff and customers heard footsteps which always approached one particular table and stopped. An experience more disturbing than disembodied footsteps was suffered by the manager at that time.

Going into the basement one evening he saw, sitting at a table, the figure of a man who appeared to be wearing the costume of a Quaker. This in itself was unnerving enough, but worse was to come, the figure had an oval mist instead of a face.

Mansfield Road, Nottingham

On occasion it seems that shades of the past encroach on the present with a specific intention, as if they are trying to reach out from the obscurity of time to inform us of some tragedy. We never seem to gain the full import of these imploring echoes — we detect only a trace or an impression, then they are gone

A good example of this are the strange events which occurred at premises on Mansfield Road, Nottingham, in 1975; then in use as an antique arms shop run by Michael Long and his staff, Bernard Shaw and Neville Kicks.

The property dates back to around 1800 and included three small cottages at the rear which Michael Long utilised as store rooms and a buffing room for renovating antique weapons. It was outside the second cottage that Bernard Shaw first encountered the ghost of a young girl one night in November 1975.

'I would estimate that she was between eight and eleven years of age, with a very pale face and large, dark eyes with her hair arranged in two bows. She wore dark clothes and a white pinafore of the style favoured in the early nineteenth century'.

'In particular I noticed she wore a pair of battered and cracked boots through which I could see her toes, but the strangest thing of all was that she appeared to have no hands'.

'There was an aura of great sadness in her demeanour and I had the impression she was trying to tell me something, although I couldn't say whether her lips moved. She then suddenly disappeared and I went back inside'.

Then Neville Kicks had an experience in the third cottage.

'I was in there one night when I developed this cold sweat and the room seemed to turn icy cold. There was a sort of chilling itch up my spine and I could have sworn there was something standing beside me. I looked twice but each time there was nothing there. It got to the pitch where I had to go outside and take a few deep breaths and, even though I didn't see anything, it was a most uncomfortable feeling'.

A few weeks later there was a break-in at the shop and an engineer was engaged to install an alarm system. Bernard Shaw takes up the story.

'One Thursday afternoon he was working next door and two of us were in the shop when we heard a banging on the wall — it was the engineer imprisoned next door'.

'What had happened was that a hook-and-eye fastening had secured the door from the outside. The engineer thought we were responsible but we assured him this was not so, as neither of us had been out there and the yard was bolted, so no-one could have been in there anyway. But due to the type of fastening the hook couldn't have dropped in place by itself'.

'After collecting some equipment from his car he went back in but once more he was trapped'.

'Letting him out again he confessed to us he was not an imaginative man but he had the strangest feeling he was not alone in there'.

Was it the presence of the girl's ghost that the engineer felt and she who was responsible for slipping the latch?

About a year later Bernard Shaw saw her once again when he went into the workshop and discovered a strange drawing on the table and standing in the corner was the girl.

As on his first encounter he gained a strong impression that she was trying to convey a message to him and there was the same aura of sadness surrounding her. But before he could approach her she had disappeared.

I can find nothing on record which would give a clue to the identity of the tragic figure which haunted these premises and I use the word 'haunted' advisedly. In order to alleviate the perturbation of his staff, Michael Long called upon the services of a reputable medium in an endeavour to lay the ghost to rest.

This seems to have worked, for the present occupants assure me that all is quiet there today. For the moment!

Roystone Fireplaces
Canal Street, Nottingham

At the beginning of this book I stated that its intention was not to prove or disprove the existence of ghosts. However, this account is a good example of a rational explanation which might well be the answer for a supposed ghost at these premises.

In 1976 members of the staff at Roystone Fireplaces Ltd. which is situated in a former police station and mortuary on Canal Street, Nottingham, were troubled by eerie and inexplicable happenings at the premises.

It began when the manager at that time arrived at work in the mornings and heard strange noises. He discovered, on several occasions, a fluorescent light burning in the corridor, which is flanked on either side by the old cells, now used for displaying fireplaces. This was confirmed by the secretary, who also heard groaning noises.

The story reached the attention of the Press and consequently Roystone Fireplaces was thronged for weeks afterwards with visitors of whom a good many claimed to be 'psychic'. They asserted that the end cell, outside which the light had been found switched on, harboured a definite 'presence'. Determined to resolve these stories one way or another, the Managing Director, Mr. Roy Parsons, decided to arrive early one morning in an endeavour to 'lay the ghost' and this is what he discovered.

'The fact that the light was found to be switched on early was due to a quick reacting fluorescent tube over-reacting before you could get into the corridor. As you came through the door and switched on the light you had to walk a few paces to get into the corridor, where you would find one single light on and one only. Then, as you switched on the lights you would hear the strange banging noise of the starter come on, but the rest of the corridor was still in darkness and I could actually get into the office before the rest of the lights came on'.

'This is what I think started the stories that the place was haunted and it was also due to a certain element of people who came down here afterwards who embellished the stories to add substance to them'.

'On the basis of conversations with policemen who were stationed here many years ago, it came to light that a body had been taken into the mortuary not dead, but in a catatonic state. It got off the slab and walked into the police station. An ambulance was called but before it arrived he died, and although this story has never been confirmed, it is my only knowledge of a death on the premises, although there no doubt have been other deaths here'.

I recently contacted the former Manager of Roystone Fireplaces and asked if in retrospect, he still believed the premises to be haunted after hearing Mr. Parsons' explanation for the ghost. To which he replied, 'Yes — there is no doubt in my mind whatsoever that those premises were haunted and perhaps still are . . . . '.

Murder at the Toll Gate

On a journey by night, snug in the comfort of ones car, when the road is deserted for miles and one seems to be the only motorist abroad, have you ever wondered what lurks in the countryside on each side of the reassuring tunnel which your headlights cut through the night? Will the road take you safely to your destination, or will something occur which will convince you of the reality of the supernatural, as it did a gentleman travelling the Great North Road on the 2nd July 1952?

He had missed the last bus from Doncaster to Retford but had managed to get a lift as far as Hawks Nest, after which he continued his journey on foot. The night was quiet save for the stirring of nocturnal creatures in the hedgerows. Mist was rising slowly from the fields on each side of the road and the moon sat in the sky on a sea of scudding cloud.

He walked down into the valley of the River Ryton and uphill again into Scrooby village. On turning the last corner, he came across a tiny cottage he had never seen before, though he knew the area well. A dim light showed at the window and, just as he began to walk by, he saw, in the shadows in the small garden, a dark figure enter the cottage. Suddenly, there was a chilling scream from within and the thudding of boots on the stairs, at which the light in the window was extinguished and a man staggered out into the garden clutching his head, his screams piercing the silence of the night. As the man fell, another figure dashed out of the cottage and vanished into the darkness. Thinking that the attacker might look for him, the onlooker ran into the fields and eventually, came back to Scrooby on the Bawtry side, where he kept to the centre of the road, hoping to find a late motorist who might stop, but the road was deserted.

In his flight he found that he had once more arrived at the spot where the cottage had stood — but it was no longer there!

Surely this could not be the spot? And yet it was; there were the same fields and hedges, but no cottage or victim lying in the garden.

As he stood there, dumbfounded, a lorry pulled up alongside and the driver, noticing that he was distressed, gave him a lift into Retford. Still in a state of shock, he went home and took to his bed.

Not surprisingly he spent a fitful night and when he did manage to sleep it was only to dream of murder, dark figures and incongruously, gibbets creaking by the roadside.

The next day he decided to report the murder to the police for surely it was murder he had seen? But how were they to believe him when the cottage and victim no longer existed?

He then returned to the location but there was still nothing to be seen. He began digging with his bare hands for he was certain that this was the spot and there, just below the surface of the grass and weeds, were revealed the mouldering foundations of an old dwelling. Incredulous at his find, he found himself a short while later wandering around Scrooby churchyard where, for some unaccountable reason, he felt compelled to examine the headstones.

He had witnessed a murder, of that he was certain but what had led him to this graveyard and for what purpose? He felt his gaze directed to a headstone projecting only inches above the ground. Most of the inscription had eroded away. Crouching down in order to see what remained of it, he discovered 'Mary — son William — murdered — 1779'.

In an effort to find an explanation, if indeed it could be explained, he examined the parish records for 1779, and this is what he discovered. 'On 3rd July 1779, William Yeadon, keeper of the Scrooby Toll Bar, and his mother, Mary Yeadon, who lived with him, were murdered and their house plundered by John Spencer of North Leverton'. The old Court registers of Nottingham tell how — 'Spencer had fractured their skulls with a hedgestake and was tried a few days later in Nottingham, then hanged at eleven o'clock on Monday 26th July 1779'.

The register then went on to say that after the hanging, the body was taken to Scrooby and hung in chains with the hedgestake in its right hand near to the place where the murder was committed.

Bessie Sheppard and Her Stone

The countryside bordering the A60 Nottingham to Mansfield road is, in parts, still thickly wooded. In the early nineteenth century it was in dense forest. It was on this forest road that fate decreed that seventeen years old Elizabeth Sheppard, whilst walking from her home in Papplewick to Mansfield in search of work, would meet her death on 7th July 1817, at the hands of a Sheffield man, Charles Rotherham.

The Bessie Stone

She had reached Harlow Wood when she encountered Rotherham, who, thinking she had money, brutally murdered her with a hedge-stake. She had no money, and Rotherham was caught ten days later at Mansfield after trying to sell her shoes and umbrella at the Three Crowns Inn at Redhill. He was executed on 28th July at Gallows Hill, Nottingham.

To ensure that the unfortunate girl's murder should not be forgotten, a Mr. Anthony Buckles together with other gentlemen of Mansfield, had a memorial stone erected on the site. This can still be seen today. The memorial is not so noticeable now, as it stands in a hollow, close to Harlow Wood Hospital, a victim of successive road improvement schemes.

Shortly after the murder, reports came from travellers and coach drivers claiming to have seen Bessie Sheppard's ghost standing by the side of the road. Today, local legend has it that whenever the memorial is moved her ghost will reappear.

As far as I can determine, the last documented sighting was in 1956, when a car involved in an accident, struck the memorial. A few nights later, a young couple travelling the road, saw an apparition, which they described as being of a young girl of medium height in a flowing white dress. It hovered over the stone for a time, then disappeared into the woods.

Trent Bridge

In the annals of ghostlore the apparition of the suicide is a prominent and persistent figure. This is hardly surprising as the taking of one's own life, whatever the circumstances. is a tragic and desparate act indeed.

Over the years many people have reported seeing strange and eerie figures in the vicinity of Trent Bridge and these are thought to be the restless images of people who chose the bridge as their exit when life became too much for them.

There have also been many legitimate, but nontheless tragic accidents on the river which may also account for these reports.

Above Ground – Airfield Ghosts

There is nothing more atmospheric and evocative of wartime England than an abandoned Royal Air Force bomber base. If you stand alone on the main runway, especially in the early evening when daylight begins to fade and the breeze sighs through the weeds in the crumbling concrete, perhaps you will hear the faint muted throb of long silenced Merlin or Hercules engines in the darkening sky. Or visit the dilapidated control tower, now silent and empty, but once a hive of activity as the bombers thundered down the runway to deliver their cargo of destruction to the heart of Germany's Ruhr; and pause for a moment to remember the many young men who took off from these airfields, never to return. They met death in many ways, all of them violent, all of them tragic. Some fell victim to night fighters others to flak, mid-air collisions in the bomber stream were not uncommon and very often the ones who did make it back succumbed to their wounds after landing. The price of our freedom was high.

It is therefore hardly surprising when considering the anguish and tragedy these airfields have witnessed, that many would seem to be haunted by ghostly figures in long-outmoded flying kit and uniforms.

Bottesford

In the cosy bar of the 'Reindeer' at Long Bennington some of the older regulars can recall when this attractive village pub was thronged with boisterous aircrews from the nearby airfield of Bottesford, situated on the Nottinghamshire/Leicestershire boundary. Should you enquire, they will tell you of a solitary figure, attired in outdated flying kit, seen many times when shadows lengthen with the onset of darkness, standing on the balcony which crowns the gaunt remains of the airfield's control tower. No one seems to know of the identity of the ghostly airman or even hazard a guess as to its nationality. Flyers of British, Australian and American units operated from Bottesford from time to time, during the Second World War.

Bottesford Airfield, Control Tower

In the 1950's the airfield was purchased by a Mr. John Rose who founded the Newark Storage Company, and the hangers were used, as they are today, as warehouses. Rumours began to circulate that the control tower was haunted. Lorry drivers on their way to the hangers reported seeing the figure of an airman on the balcony, and they were able to observe it long enough to note that the chin strap on its flying helmet was unfastened. It would then disappear.

Not only does the control tower appear to be haunted but also one of the hangers. One evening a few years ago a lorry driver, after unloading his vehicle, decided to take a stroll. As he approached one of the hangers, he heard the sound of a multi engined aircraft being 'revved up' inside, together with voices and laughter. Somewhat puzzled by this, he opened a small door in the side of the hangar and peered inside. Although the sounds continued, the hanger remained empty. He lost no time in getting back to his vehicle.

With permission from the Newark Storage Company, the Nottingham Psychical Research Group were able to spend the night of October 26th 1985 at the control tower. As the night progressed a blanket of mist enveloped the airfield. When viewed from the top of the tower the area took on a mysterious aspect, and it was very easy to imagine the bombers with their exhausted crews returning to the airfield after a raid over four decades ago.

Unfortunately the night we had chosen for our investigation proved to be exceptionally cold. In spite of the warmth provided by sleeping bags and the contents of vacuum flasks, the cold drove us out. We descended the tower's dog-leg staircase with Roy in the lead, followed in less than two minutes by Bob and myself.

On this occasion I had travelled with Roy, and as we left the airfield I was surprised when this astute Yorkshireman confessed that whilst waiting at the bottom of the staircase he had felt uneasy. He had sensed an atmosphere of forboding, which he had not felt earlier.

Shortly after our investigation at Bottesford we held one of our regular meetings. Bob and me arrived first, and I was taken aback when he declared that whilst waiting for me to descend the staircase he became aware of a 'presence' behind him. He kept glancing over his shoulder but there was nothing to be seen and he was relieved to get out of the building. Both Bob and Roy have been members of the Group for a number of years and this was the first time that either of them had commented on feeling uneasy. It was decided that we should return to Bottesford in the near future.

Langar

Remembered locally for its post war association with the Royal Canadian Air Force and now an industrial estate, Langar saw little operational service during the war. It was first used as a satellite for Bottesford and later by A. V. Roe as a repair depot for damaged Lancasters. From September 1942 to October 1943 however the airfield was used in an operational capacity by the Lancasters of No. 207 Squadron Royal Air Force. They participated in many major raids. Today, many of the wartime buildings remain, such as the control tower which is now used by the British Parachute School, and the former Officers' Mess, transformed into business premises for Shortland Crafts.

One night in 1983, Mr. Keith Shortland (a director of Shortland Crafts) had secured the premises and was driving away when he encountered a tall, uniformed figure which appeared in front of his car. Thinking that he had run the man over, Mr. Shortland stopped his car. A search revealed no-one and assuming it to be some form of optical illusion, he dismissed the incident from his mind. The same thing recurred some weeks later under similar circumstances, and he realised that the figure must have been a phantom. Mr. Shortland had the impression that the ghost was standing guard, was not malevolent and sensed that he would not see it again. He later learnt from local people that when the Canadians were stationed at Langar there was a tragic accident involving a bomb, and several airmen were killed. This might have accounted for the apparition, or was the figure a crewman of 207 Squadron, who did not return from operations? One of the 55,000 aircrew lost by Bomber Command during World War Two.

Below Ground – Colliery Ghosts

In common with other hazardous occupations the coal extractive industry has had its fatalities over the years, especially before the rigorous safety standards of today were imposed. In all probability it is due to these fatal accidents that there are so many tales of ghosts at the collieries.

The average miner is renowned for being a pragmatic man and yet the reports of ghosts seen in today's highly mechanised mines are nearly as frequent as in the days of the pick and shovel.

Admittedly the miners' working environment is a dark and shadowy one, but these men are used to such conditions, thus all the reports cannot be dismissed as tricks of the light or other such explanations.

Here then, are some ghost stories from the Nottinghamshire coalfield.

Clipstone Colliery

In 1984, in a remote section of this colliery, two young miners fled in terror after an encounter with a ghost attired in the working clothes and safety helmet of the type now on display in the museum of mining history.

One of the miners said, 'It put a hand on my shoulder and I just froze. Afterwards I was hysterical'.

Officials at the colliery decided that the two miners should not work alone for a while.

Babbington Colliery

Mr. R. C. Green of Aspley, now in his late forties, has been a miner since leaving school at the age of fifteen. For many years he has worked at Babbington Colliery where he and his colleagues have experienced numerous encounters with the paranormal.

In 1954, Mr. Green was working an afternoon shift with four colleagues engaged in walling off an unworkable section of the mine. Whilst taking a break, the miners saw emerging from a small aperture in the wall a figure attired not in the orange overalls of today's miner, but in the rough working clothes of yesteryear. The figure stood with arms folded as if inspecting their work. One of the miners approached the figure but before he could reach it, it turned and disappeared back into the old workings.

Mr. Green had an equally strange experience whilst working a night shift some years later. He was nearing the end of his shift and was preparing to leave when he had a feeling that he was not alone. Suddenly, a man appeared out of the gloom and Mr. Green saw that his features were badly mutilated. The horrific figure did not stop and, shambling on its way, was soon lost to sight. Subsequent enquiries by Mr. Green revealed that many years before, a miner had been killed at that location in an accident involving a cutting machine.

A well known story is told at Babbington of a miner who had difficulty in opening two heavy doors in one of the old workings. He managed to open the first door but not the second. As he struggled with this door, he heard an echoing voice from behind it say, 'I'll give you a hand'. The door easily swung open but no-one was revealed behind it. This is, I am told, a section of the colliery where many miners have heard voices and laughter, a search revealed nothing to account for them.

Mr. Green recalls another inexplicable incident at the colliery when a colleague saw a strange figure walk into the cage at the bottom of the shaft. But later, when talking to the engineer, his colleague learned that when the cage reached the surface and the doors were opened, it was empty.

Perhaps one of the strangest stories to come from Babbington was told by a team of miners who had finished a night shift. On their way to board the cage en route to the surface, they saw a figure wearing a flat cap and waistcoat, the traditional apparel of the old miners, but who, in contrast to his dusty ragged clothes sported a brilliant white scarf. As the miners approached the figure it disappeared. Lying on the ground at the spot where it had stood, was found the tattered remains of a once white scarf.

Most of the collieries in Nottinghamshire have their ghosts but Babbington, possibly because it is one of the oldest, seems to have more than most. Mr. Green however is not afraid of his spectral workmates for he feels that the spirits of these long dead miners do not constitute a threat to the welfare of miners today.

ACKNOWLEDGEMENTS

I would like to acknowledge with gratitude all the people whose help and co-operation made this book possible.

Mr. and Mrs. B. Baines, Mr. B. Birchenall of the Nottingham County Council, Mr. A. Bush, Mr. D. Cantrill, Mr. and Mrs. D. Cupitt, Mr. A. Freeman, Mr. R. C. Green, the Reverend T. Hoyle, Mr. N. Kicks, Mr. M. Long, Mr. and Mrs. J. Lowe, Mrs. L. Mills, Nancy, Mr. R. Parsons, Mr. and Mrs. Price, Mr. J. Rose, Mr. B. Shaw, Mr. K. Shortland, Mrs. L. and Mr. P. Wishall, Mr. D. W. Wright.

I am indebted to the Editor of the Retford Times Mr. A. V. Illger for allowing me to present 'Murder at the Toll Gate' which is based on a story which appeared in a 1952 issue of this publication entitled 'The Ghost of Scrooby Toll Gate'. Also to the Editor of the Nottingham Evening Post for permission to quote from an item about the Little London Herbal Stores.

My special thanks go to Mr. B. Loughbrough, Arts Director of the Nottingham City Council and of course 'the team' — Jack Lumsden, Roy Westerman, Robert Sisson and Malcolm Crozier. In addition I wish to thank Malcolm for supplying the photographs for this book, Peter J. Naylor for his considerable help and expertise as Editor, and a big thank you to my wife Jeanette for her encouragement, patience and understanding during its writing.

The Ghosts & Legends Series-

DERBYSHIRE & THE PEAK DISTRICT -

DERBYSHIRE GHOSTS by Wayne Anthony Boylan . ISBN 0 946404 67 4

STRANGE TALES OF THE PEAK by Richard Lichfield. ISBN.0 946404

THE ADVENTURES OF A BAKEWELL GOBLIN by Ben Andrews.

FURTHER ADVENTURES OF A BAKEWELL GOBLIN by Ben Andrews

PEAK DISTRICT MONSTERS by Alan Smith.

LEGENDS OF DERBYSHIRE by John N. Merrill

DERBYSHIRE FOLKLORE by John N. Merrill

CUSTOMS OF DERBYSHIRE & THE PEAK DISTRICT by John N. Merrill

NOTTINGHAMSHIRE -

GHOST HUNTING AROUND NOTTINGHAMSHIRE by Rosemary Robb . ISBN 0 946404

GHOSTS & LEGENDS OF NEWARK by Rosemary Robb. ISBN 0 946404

THE RESTLESS SPIRIT - more ghosts and legends - by Rosemary Robb

THE GHOSTS OF WOLLATON HALL by Keith Taylor. ISBN 0 946404

HAUNTED NOTTINGHAMSHIRE - Vol 1 - by Len Moakes . ISBN 0 946404 31 3

HAUNTED NOTTINGHAMSHIRE - Vol 2 - by Len Moakes . ISBN 0 946404 72 0

PHANTOM HIGHWAYMEN AND SPECTURAL COACHES by Len Moakes

NOTTINGHAMSHIRE RAILWAY GHOSTS by John R. Smalley . ISBN 0 946404

LINCOLNSHIRE -

HAUNTED LINCOLNSHIRE by Sean Mcneaney

The Nottinghamshire Heritage Series -

BELL TALES by Stan Smith
SOME NOTTINGHAMSHIRE PUB STORIES by Stan Smith
RHYME AND REASON - some Nottinghamshire Folk Tales by Stan Smith

FOR CONSPICUOUS GALLANTRY - Local V.C. Holders - by N. McCrery

HISTORY OF SUTTON IN ASHFIELD - facsimile of 1907 edition

LORD BYRON" Mad, bad and dangerous to know."- by E. Eisenberg

NOTTINGHAMSHIRE STREET TO STREET GUIDE .

THE OLD NORTH ROAD by Joan Board
A TO Z OF PILGRIM COUNTRY by Joan Board

WOLLATON HALL by Elizabeth May
Wollaton as a family home and Natural History Museum

COUNTRY POETRY by Leslie Williamson

NOTTINGHAM IN VERSE - "The Soul of the City" by Alsion Davies

MARY & WILLIAM - a north Midland couple by Joy Dunicliff

BASFORD - Village to Suburb by A.S.Bowley
RAILWAYS REMEMBERED - Basford & Bulwell - 1848 - 1967 by Ashley R. Durose.

LOOKING UP AT NOTTINGHAM - 9 historical city walks by Terence White

For a free catalog of titles
- more than 300 - please write to -

Walk & Write Ltd.,
Unit 1, Molyneux Business Park,
Whitworth Road, Darley Dale,
Matlock, Derbyshire. DE4 2HJ